# The Fighting Gamecock

# The
# Fighting
# Gamecock

★ ★ ★

## Idella Bodie

**SANDLAPPER PUBLISHING CO., INC.**

ORANGEBURG, SOUTH CAROLINA

Published by Sandlapper Publishing Co., Inc.
Orangeburg, South Carolina

Manufactured in the United States of America

Second Printing, 2002

**Library of Congress Cataloging-in-Publication Data**

Bodie, Idella.
    The fighting gamecock / Idella Bodie.
        p. cm. — (Heroes and heroines of the American Revolution)
    Includes bibliographical references.
    Summary: Traces the life of General Thomas Sumter, whose guerrilla
tactics during the Revolutionary War helped American colonists win their
independence from Great Britain.
    ISBN 0-87844-151-4
    1. Sumter, Thomas, 1734-1832—Juvenile literature. 2. Generals—
United States—Biography—Juvenile literature. 3. United States.
Continental Army—Biography—Juvenile literature. 4. South Carolina—
Militia—Biography—Juvenile literature. 5. United States—History—
Revolution, 1775-1783—Campaigns—Juvenile literature. [1. Sumter,
Thomas, 1734-1832. 2. Generals. 3. United States—History—Revolution,
1775-1783.] I. Title.

E207.S95 B63 2000
973.3'457'092—dc21
[B]

00-022289

In spring of 1780 THOMAS SUMTER galloped from his home in the High Hills to recruit a band of backwoodsmen in the Up Country of South Carolina. Darting out from secret bases, he and his guerrilla troops ambushed the enemy at fords and ferries along the Catawba and Wateree Rivers. Like a fighting ğamecock he pit himself and his men against mightier British forces.

# How Thomas Sumter Got His Nickname

When General Sumter rode into North Carolina seeking money, rifles, and men for his volunteer militia, he decided to visit a family of famous rifle makers living near the Blue Ridge Mountains.

The Gillespie brothers were rugged backwoodsmen whose favorite pastime was cockfighting. When Sumter reached their forge, he found the brothers crouched around a cockpit admiring their blue game hens. Old Tuck, who never lost a fight, had produced chicks known throughout the Carolina mountains. None had ever drawn back from a fight or shown a white feather.

Sumter began to bargain for rifles, and the brothers praised his courage in joining a struggle as hopeless as the Revolutionary War.

Sumter stood his ground, handsome and fit in his blue coat with scarlet facings and golden epaulettes. A cock feather jutted up from his hat.

"You know," one of the brothers said, "Thomas looks just like Old Tuck."

Before long the Carolinas rang with the nickname "Gamecock."

adapted from *The Gamecock: The Life and Campaigns of General Thomas Sumter* by Robert D. Bass

# To the Young Reader

Like Francis Marion, the Swamp Fox, Thomas Sumter was leader of a band of Carolina volunteers in the American Revolution. Also like Marion, he learned his brand of fighting in the French and Indian War on the American frontier.

During a series of Carolina campaigns, British cavalry officer Banastre Tarleton and Sumter pecked away at each other. Tarleton, commander of the Green Dragoons, once told his men, "We'll never catch that 'swamp fox.' Let's go back and pick a fight with the 'gamecock.'"

Sumter, however, gave Tarleton a hard time too. A daring and powerful leader, he told Light Horse Harry Lee he would "wade through blood" to win.

In your reading about these heroes and heroines of the Revolutionary War, I hope you will discover their personalities are as different as those of persons everywhere.

# Contents

# 1.
# Preddy's Creek, Virginia

Thomas was glad to be away from the meadow where he had watched his family's sheep all day long.

Now that their evening meal was over, he listened to his mother's stories of the "Old World," the name she gave her homeland of England.

Of all the children Thomas loved his mother's stories best. He was also the most like her, with his blue eyes, brown hair, soaring imagination, and strong will.

In his mind Thomas could see the pictures his mother painted with her words of British gentlemen and ladies with their gracious manners. He longed for the day he could look as dashing in a ruffled shirt and handsome breeches.

Thomas knew his mother, Patience, had grown up in a genteel society. She had been given a fine education and wanted as much for her children. Unfortunately that was not to be.

As a young woman Patience fell in love with a poor young man, married him, and sailed with him to America. Her new life was difficult.

When her hardworking husband died at an early age, Patience—still without children—married William Sumter, another English emigrant.

To find free land, the couple moved to Preddy's Creek, a settlement in Louisa County, Virginia. At the foot of a mountain along the Blue Ridge, they built a cabin and began farming. William also built a gristmill on the Rivanna River.

Like their neighbors, the Sumters struggled to make a living.

Patience and William had four children. Mrs. Sumter was a caring and attentive mother. The children, too young to work on the farm, attended a nearby school. On Sundays the family went to church together.

When Thomas was old enough, his father put him to work in their gristmill. High-spirited Thomas was always singing and dancing around in his leather breeches.

No matter what Thomas did with his friends, he insisted on being the leader. He was the strongest swimmer among them and always won when they wrestled or played a game called "fives."

When Thomas's father died, his mother had no way to make a living to support her children.

She had no choice but to bind Thomas to a farmer named Benjamin Cave who needed strong boys to plow his fields.

Like Lucas, another of the plowboys, Thomas had only one shirt. On Sundays the boys washed their shirts in Cave's Creek and hung them on bushes to dry. While their shirts dried, they played marbles.

Most of the men who lived along Preddy's Creek were farmers and woodsmen. Many of them could not read and write. They spent much of their free time watching cockfights.

Thomas and Lucas were often in the company of these crude, rough men. The boys even had their own gamecocks.

Thomas's mother may not have been aware her son was being exposed to a life so different from her own upbringing. There was, however, talk among neighbors that her slender, muscular son gambled and joined in cockfighting.

After hearing all the rumors, pretty neighborhood girls would have nothing to do with Thomas. When he strutted by their houses like one of the gamecocks he fought, they tossed their heads and flounced off.

Before long, however, Thomas found a career that changed his life.

# 2.
# Becoming a Soldier

In Virginia where Sumter was growing up, the Indians were friendly and helpful to the settlers. In other places Indians tried to drive the colonists off lands that had been their hunting grounds for thousands of years. Terrible fighting broke out.

At the same time the English and French were sending troops to America to fight each other for land. Both sides had strong support from Indian tribes. The colonists called the series of battles the French and Indian War.

Indians began to move along the Blue Ridge Mountains, murdering, scalping, and burning. Colonel George Washington called for regiments to be organized against them. Sumter signed up to train with Colonel William Byrd.

After a summer of camping, hiking, and training in the wilderness, Sumter found he enjoyed the activity and excitement of military life. His regiment headed for Ohio where they captured a French fort and renamed it Fort Pitt.

By the end of this campaign, Sumter's leadership, bravery, and willingness to take dangerous assignments earned him the rank of sergeant. Finally the English had won.

After their victory, the English agreed the Indians should have claim to the western lands. An order was sent out among the colonists forbidding them from settling west of the Appalachian Mountains. Land there was to be reserved for the Indians.

The English hoped this would prevent fighting between the colonists and the Indians, but some settlers refused to obey the proclamation. The Cherokees went on the warpath.

Colonel Byrd's regiment was sent to fight the Cherokees. Before the Virginians could get involved in the fight, militias from the Carolinas destroyed Indian villages, killing so many warriors old Chief Kanagatucko called for an end to fighting.

The chief traveled to the capital at Williamsburg to discuss a peace treaty. When an agreement was reached, Chief Kanagatucko asked that a Virginian carry the document to his people. The colonel in charge refused, saying, "I will not send one of my men on such a dangerous mission." The chief returned home.

High-spirited Sumter heard what had happened and volunteered to take the treaty to the Indians. With a lieutenant and an interpreter, he set out on what became a hard nineteen-day trip by land and water to Cherokee country.

As the men neared their destination, they were stopped by Indians bearing rifles. "To what town do you belong?" a Cherokee shouted.

"The English camp," the interpreter replied.

"The English and Cherokee have made peace. We are carrying the treaty to the Cherokee nation."

The Indians lowered their rifles and invited the Virginians to their camp. With great friendliness the Cherokees served a supper of dried venison, honey, and boiled corn. Afterwards they directed  the three men to Chief Kanagatucko.

Sumter had a curious mind. He was always eager to increase his knowledge by observing manners and customs of others. He was especially interested in the way the Indians dressed. While he listened to their songs, he observed the beads, shells, and feathers decorating their clothing. He saw, too, the pride they took in the care of their weapons.

After watching the Indians' athletic contests, Sumter decided he could outrun, outshoot, and outwrestle any brave among the Cherokees. They allowed him to join in their games. Like most men brought up around Indians, Sumter knew some of their words. Now he learned more.

Two months later when the soldiers started home, the new Indian friends sent a party of one hundred men to guard them on their journey.

# 3.
# A Trip Abroad

In Williamsburg the governor of Virginia entertained Indian Chief Ostenaco and showed him a picture of King George III of England.

"Long have I wished to see the King, my father," the chief told him.

The governor decided to do something about Chief Ostenaco's wish. He engaged Sumter and Timberlake, an interpreter, to escort three Indian chiefs to London.

The visit of the American Indians filled London with excitement. People gathered around these tall, bronzed-skin men whose clothing and heads were decorated with shells, feathers, and earrings.

Sumter and Timberlake wanted to get in on the excitement. They bought scarlet coats worn by the British officers and pretended they were officers rather than ordinary soldiers. As the Cherokees' escorts, the two men received invitations to all the important places in London.

Crowds always gathered to see the Indians. One evening, Sumter was surprised to find servants at one home they visited charging admission. He became so angry he knocked a servant down. It was time to go home.

Back in America, Sumter escorted the chiefs to their villages. Before leaving to return home, Sumter captured a French lieutenant who came to the camp to try to talk the Cherokees into fighting against the English. Sumter tied the man on his horse, mounted behind him, and carried him to Fort Prince George.

Leaving his prisoner in Virginia, Sumter made his way down through the Carolinas. He liked the people of the Carolina frontier. Many Virginians had already settled there.

When he reached Eutaw Springs, he stopped. Three miles south of the murmuring springs the road forked toward Nelson's Ferry.

"What a sight for a store!" he said to himself as he looked around. Then he reined his horse toward Charleston.

After being paraded as a hero in Charleston, Sumter headed back toward Virginia, stopping one more time to look at the land around Nelson's Ferry.

Thomas Sumter was twenty-nine years old. He had spent the last seven years in military service.

At home in Preddy's Creek he found that his mother was now a skilled midwife and his brother and sisters were married. Mrs. Sumter beamed as her son told of his adventures in England, the land of her birth.

Sumter enjoyed being with his family, but he was eager to move on.

Before he had a chance to leave, he found himself in jail. An angry man who loaned Sumter money for the peace treaty trip wanted to be repaid. Sumter argued that the government still owed him, but the man would not listen.

An old friend visited him in his jail cell and left behind a tomahawk and ten guineas. Using one or both, Sumter escaped.

Three weeks later he rode into the settlement of Long Canes Creek on the frontier between Cherokee land and South Carolina.

# 4.
# Family Man

In the little settlement of Long Canes Creek, Sumter tried to decide what he should do. Should he return to Virginia? Or should he stay in South Carolina?

The Cherokees loved him. He could be an Indian trader and become rich. The governor of South Carolina respected him. Besides, land was free from the Blue Ridge Mountains to the sea islands.

He vaulted into his saddle and headed down the Cherokee Path toward Charleston. He rode through communities on the Saluda and Congaree Rivers and stopped for a while at Eutaw Springs.

He liked the land and the creek flowing past dogwoods, poplars, and oaks.

In Charleston the British government at last paid Sumter for his work with the Indians. With the money he bought land at Eutaw Springs, in St. John's Parish, and built a small store. He stocked the store with items needed by people living in the area.

The spot proved to be a good location for a store. Nearby plantations, the transportation of goods by land, and Santee River traffic soon made him prosperous. He began to buy more land.

Summers were hot on the plantations, and mosquitoes often caused deadly illnesses. During a yellow fever epidemic a neighboring planter, William Jameson, died. Jameson's wife, Mary, stayed on in their home.

As soon as Sumter felt it proper, he visited his

friend's widow. Mary, who had suffered polio as a child, liked the handsome storekeeper and enjoyed his stories of living with the Indians and visiting London. She had heard from neighbors how Thomas could swim the rolling Santee River and vault into his saddle without touching his horse or stirrup. Knowing nothing of his wild younger days, gentle, good-natured Mary saw him as serious and hardworking.

Thomas and Mary married. Mary shared her wealth and plantation on the Great Savannah north of the Santee River swamp with her new husband. The couple had four children, William, Thomas, Patience, and Anne.

Remembering his boyhood days, Sumter built a gristmill and a sawmill on Jack's Creek.

For the Sumters, life was good, but times were becoming troubled for the colonies. Talk spread of breaking away from England.

Sumter considered himself a Loyalist. He had been to England and met King George. Why, he wondered, should he fight against him?

During a summer trip to Charleston to get supplies for his store, something happened that

changed Sumter's mind. He heard a fiery speech made by Christopher Gadsden under a tree, later called the Liberty Tree. Gadsden's words sparked a flame of liberty in his heart.

From that time on Sumter was dedicated to the independence of America. He was among the first of the Patriots to take up the fight for freedom in South Carolina.

# 5.
# Frustration

Sumter rode his horse over the countryside, repeating Christopher Gadsden's words: "The American colonies must stand together in fighting for their rights!"

People, especially those of the Up Country, liked what Sumter had to say. They liked it so much they elected him to the first Provincial Congress of South Carolina.

One January day Sumter gathered with other Patriot delegates in Charleston. They talked about how they might deal with Loyalists, Americans who had taken the side of the British. They also discussed problems they would face with their

British appointed governor, Lord William Campbell.

Tension increased and Americans began to fight among themselves.

Since Sumter had fought in the Virginia militia in earlier years, he was asked to form a volunteer company of Patriot soldiers. He lost no time in rounding up neighboring farmers.

The first assignment of his militia was to aid Colonel Richard Richardson in capturing Tory leaders in the Ninety Six area. A two-day battle there resulted in the death of James Birmingham, the first South Carolinian to be killed in the Revolutionary War.

Back at camp winter weather made their duties difficult. "For eight days," Colonel Richardson reported later, "we never had a place to lie down, for a deep snow covered the ground.

Finally, a cold rain fell, together with sleet. It melted the snow, causing every creek and river to flood its bank."

Many soldiers suffered frostbite as they were poorly clothed and their shoes had worn out.

However, this Snow Campaign, as the

incident came to be called, was a victory for Sumter. On his trip to take the peace treaty to the Cherokees he had worn frozen clothes and slept on wet blankets. That experience had prepared him for this one.

In spite of the weather, the mission was accomplished, and the soldiers would return home. The Patriots had captured over a hundred Loyalists. Upon reaching the Congaree River swamp, Colonel Richardson turned the prisoners over to Sumter who took them under guard to Nelson's Ferry.

When the colonel made his report, he wrote,

"Captain Thomas Sumter has given extra service to me and to the country."

After a few days of rest at home with Mary and their children, Sumter rode on to Charleston. There, Congress commissioned him a lieutenant colonel and put him in charge of the Second Regiment of Riflemen.

Sumter set off at once to recruit sharp-shooting settlers and Indians. The company of recruits camped at Ten Mile Spring while Sumter trained them. During the training he spoke often to his men of bravery.

Sumter's first assignment for his riflemen did not involve fighting. Instead, they guarded the city of Charleston. Later, they watched the battle of Sullivan's Island from a distance in case the British might try to land troops. Afterwards, Sumter's troops marched under the burden of a thousand pounds of gunpowder being delivered to Colonel Williamson's militia in the Blue Ridge Mountains. They guarded a supply depot and performed other dull duties. During all this time Sumter was restless for action.

The only excitement Sumter had felt, he decided, was on the day he led his horsemen across a fourteen-foot-wide ledge of rock in the Blue Ridge Mountains. The Chestatee River lay sixty feet below them.

Sumter was frustrated. He had hoped to be celebrated because of fighting in battles, but he had only seen others win the glory. To make matters worse, he contracted malaria and became so ill he had to return home.

# 6.
# Liberty or Death

When spring came, Sumter moved his family to their summer home on the bank of the Wateree River. The area was known as the High Hills of Santee because of the high sand hills along the east bank of the river. Being away from the heat and mosquitoes improved Sumter's health as well as Mary's.

By that time British officers Lord Cornwallis and Colonel Banastre Tarleton had heard of the capturing of Tories in the Snow Campaign. They were determined to find and punish Sumter for his part in the act.

Lord Rawdon, another British officer, offered

a reward for Sumter's capture. "I will give a large sum of money to any man who will lead Sumter into a British ambush," he announced.

Tory soldiers were afraid of Sumter's strength and his daring way of fighting. No one would take up the challenge.

Banastre Tartleton, or "Bloody Ban," as the Patriots called him for his cruelty, raced along the Santee River slashing anything and everything in his path. He slaughtered farm animals and burned homes and outbuildings. He even killed enemy soldiers after they waved the white flag of surrender.

One morning young Tom, Sumter's son, was riding through the warm High Hills. Suddenly a frightened neighbor galloped past, yelling, "Tartleton's headed this way! He's after your father!"

Tom raced home, his breath hot and dry, to shout the warning.

When Sumter heard the news, he stood tall and clinched his jaw in determination. He knew what he had to do. He put on his uniform from his days as colonel of the Sixth Regiment and kissed Mary and his children goodbye.

"Soldier Tom," he called to his old friend and faithful slave, "saddle our horses."

From that day forward Sumter adopted the call "liberty or death!"

A short time after Sumter's departure, Tartleton and his dragoons rode in a wild rage up to the Sumter home. Finding the Patriot gone, the British soldiers plundered the house and then set it on fire.

# 7.
# Rocky Mount

When Sumter heard his home had been burned, he was more determined than ever to fight. He and Soldier Tom galloped northward along the Wateree and Catawba Rivers where he met many veterans of his old Sixth Regiment. These men had not lost their desire for freedom or their will to fight. They were in need of a leader. Now they had one.

Sumter began to develop a plan. He would recruit these volunteers and others and fight a guerrilla war. With his men he would lurk in the swamp along the Catawba River. From their hiding place they would burst out to burn lands and homes of Tories and kill British troops as they crossed the ferries and fords.

The commander of the southern army, General Horatio Gates, approved Sumter's plan. The Gamecock gathered his scouts. "We must know the position of every British officer," he told them. "I'm assigning men to watch bridges and ferries."

Scattered bands of other Carolinians heard Sumter was back in the war. Knowing that the colonel was an experienced officer, they approached him. "Will you be our leader too?" they asked. Some Tory soldiers even crossed over to the Patriot side.

"We have made the same promise to ourselves," he told them. "With me as with you, it is liberty or death."

Sumter's scouts reported that British troops held a post at Rocky Mount. Tories established

the fort by taking over two log houses and a board building. They dug a deep ditch around the structures. Then they cut down trees, sharpened the ends of branches, and poked them outward from the ditch. This barricade, called an abatis, would keep the enemy from crossing the moat.

Sumter had learned that for once his men outnumbered the British. When they reached the enemy camp at Rocky Mount, they settled in behind a nearby ledge of rocks. Sumter called out, demanding that the Tories surrender. They refused.

Soon, the air burst with rifle fire. To the

amazement of the Patriots, their rifle balls would not go through the walls of the buildings.

The Gamecock ordered several men to charge across the yard and fire from closer range. Still their ammunition would not penetrate. Before a colonel and seven privates could take cover, they were killed by British snipers.

Quick with another plan, Sumter directed his men to light pieces of kindling and throw them

onto the rooftop of the smallest house. That fire, he told them, would spread to the other buildings. In spite of the danger of the mission, two soldiers volunteered to toss the lighted kindling. A boulder one hundred yards from their rock ledge seemed the best place from which to throw the torches.

In order to protect the volunteers from deadly British fire as they ran to the boulder, comrades covered their chests and backs with slender pieces of firewood. Then they tied them in place with a strong cord and filled the runners' arms with bundles of kindling.

As the volunteers dashed toward the boulder, Patriots bombarded the buildings with rifle fire.

Working frantically behind the boulder, the men sparked a fire. Soon flaming firebrands hurled toward the building.

Flames flared; smoke billowed.

Then the unexpected happened. Thunder roared and lightning flashed. Rain beat down, flooding the battleground and choking the flames.

Sumter had no choice but to withdraw his men. The Patriots had lost the battle of Rocky Mount to a thunderstorm!

The colonel learned later the British had refused to surrender because they knew Patriot musket balls could not penetrate the extra wall of logs they had placed inside the house.

Sumter was never discouraged by defeat. Soon, he would decide where his militia would strike next.

# 8.
# Hanging Rock

The following Sunday morning the Gamecock chose Hanging Rock as the Patriots' next target. Scouts reported that British officers had pulled infantrymen away from this camp for another assignment. Without those soldiers, Sumter knew Hanging Rock would be weak. By evening of that same day his regiment was on its way.

Rains had swollen the red water of the Catawba River. As Sumter and his troops crossed, currents swept men and horses downstream.

Finally, wet and discouraged, the Patriots gathered on the other side of the river. Some had lost horses; others, rifles.

But Sumter rallied them on, and by morning they had covered the sixteen miles of ruts and mud to Hanging Rock.

As its name suggests, a huge boulder jutted out over the high creek bank, forming a perfect shelter for the British camp.

A scout reported the enemy troops had just finished breakfast and men were scattering to do morning chores. At this good news, Sumter's Patriots made a surprise attack. Some Tories fled into nearby woods. Others grabbed rifles and charged.

Shots rang out. Bayonets flashed against the sunlight, cold and deadly. The battle became bitter hand-to-hand combat.

The Gamecock galloped recklessly amid the battle. With his hair flying and his golden epaulettes shining, he made a perfect target for enemy sharpshooters. Still, he shouted commands and praise to his men.

Like Old Tuck, the most courageous of the fighting cocks, Sumter made no sound when a rifle ball ripped into his thigh. He continued to ride, directing the fight.

When their supplies ran low, Sumter's men gathered rifles and ammunition from the dead. Before long, they had pushed the British back, but bodies of the dead and dying from both sides lay strewn over the battlefield.

With British officers gone and prisoners taken, Sumter's men began to loot the British camp. They were battle-weary, thirsty, and hungry. The temptation of food and rum was too much. Before long, some were unfit for duty.

Sumter gave orders to make litters for the wounded, take anything needed from the British camp, and prepare for retreat. With some wagons loaded with the dead and wounded and others with plunder from the British camp, the Patriots set out. Their withdrawal ended in a camp at Waxhaws.

After the men had settled into camp and night fell, Sumter called Soldier Tom to dress the wound in his thigh.

"I'm swearing you to secrecy," he told his old friend. "It would not be good for my men to know I have been shot."

Before turning in, Sumter wrote a long report of the Rocky Mount and Hanging Rock battles to be sent to General Gates. He did not mention his injury.

# 9.
# Fishing Creek

As always, General Gates was impressed with Sumter's reports. His return message read, "Move down the Catawba and Wateree Rivers. Seize all fords and close the ferries."

Over many days and nights Sumter's men made the long march along the rivers under Gates's orders.

Sweeping down the Wateree, they captured wagons loaded with corn, rum, and other supplies. Along the way they plundered Tory property and took cattle and sheep.

All of this plunder, as well as prisoners taken, slowed down their march, which was already long and weary. Yet Sumter refused to give up the stolen property.

British colonel Tarleton heard of Sumter's slow-moving troops. "If only I can crush the Gamecock," he said to himself, "it would bring my campaign to a glorious end."

Sumter learned that Tarleton's troops were tracking him. His goal was to stay a safe distance ahead. When the Patriots reached Fishing Creek, forty miles north of Camden, Sumter believed that his men had advanced far enough to stop for rest. "We'll camp here," he said.

The tired militia celebrated the good news. They stacked their muskets and rifles against the wagons. Some ate. Others drank rum, swam in the creek, or went to sleep.

Exhausted from herding his troops, Sumter passed his command to another officer. He tossed his hat with the cock's feather on the ground, laid his blue coat aside, and pulled off his boots. Then he stretched out on a blanket in the shade of a wagon.

When Tarleton's scouts reported Sumter had camped at Fishing Creek, the British colonel urged his cavalry and infantry on. They carried with them a fieldpiece, a lightweight cannon.

By nightfall the British could see the soft glow of Patriot campfires on the opposite side of the creek. Tarleton ordered his men not to light fires and to remain quiet.

At first light of day British troops crossed the creek. Advancing around the bend, they met with Sumter's watchmen. One of the Patriots on guard opened fire, killing a dragoon. In response, the two watchmen were killed.

Sumter heard the shots and called out,

demanding the cause.

"It's some of our militia killing cattle for food," an officer reassured him.

Since that was a common practice in camps, Sumter saw no cause for alarm.

Tarleton's shout to advance his charge came as a complete surprise to the waking camp. Patriots scattered to the woods or dashed to swim the river. A few tried to grab guns, but it was too late.

Sumter recognized the terror spreading through the camp. He saw Tarleton's troops between his men and their stacked rifles. Officers and soldiers fell under deadly swords.

The Gamecock sprang up, cut the halter of a wagon horse, and vaulted onto the animal's back. Shouting orders, he tried to rally his remaining men. It was no use. He saw one of his officers

running toward the swamp. They had lost the fight. To avoid capture, he took off in a gallop.

When he was out of range of the musket balls, Sumter looked back. At that moment his horse lumbered, and his head crashed into a large oak limb.

When he regained consciousness, night had fallen and his horse was gone. Wandering in the dark, he was a general without an army. He had lost a large number of men and all of the troop's provisions.

Finally, he reached the home of friends, the Barnetts. Standing at the door, without hat, coat, or boots, he knocked.

"Do, Mrs. Barnett," he said, "let me have something to eat, if only a piece of johnny cake or a glass of milk."

Mrs. Barnett invited him in.

The following morning Thomas Sumter joined the stream of people fleeing danger and made his way to a Patriot camp.

Tarleton's troops had won the battle of Fishing Creek. But for the British commander, it was not a victory because the Gamecock had escaped.

"If Sumter had not removed his coat because of the heat," Tarleton was heard to say, "my men would have recognized him. He would be dead now or at least taken prisoner."

In spite of the embarrassing defeat, a week later the Gamecock had reorganized his regiment and gained new recruits. Once again he patrolled the rivers.

Fortunately, he had given his bag with important papers, cash, and certificates to Soldier Tom. In one of the sweeps downriver, they recovered the bag from a bush where Soldier Tom had hidden it.

Sumter had made a comeback.

# 10.
# Blackstock's

The Gamecock, now commissioned as brigadier general by Governor Rutledge, camped on the Enoree River. He was sending out raiding parties when he heard Tarleton wanted to pick a fight. Sumter was not afraid, but he was concerned about his militia facing the charge of the powerful British dragoons.

His men did not fear muskets or rifles. They were familiar with firearms and had seen men recover after being shot by accident while hunting. But they were afraid to face the cold steel of British bayonets. And there was the British cannon fire.

Sumter called together his colonels. They too were ready to fight—*if* they could take a position behind some strong protection.

One of the officers suggested Patriot captain William Blackstock's plantation. "Besides the woods and fences," he said, "there are buildings on the hill above the Tyger River."

With plans laid, Sumter's men forded the Enoree River and headed to Blackstock's.

When Sumter saw the layout of the land, he knew his men would have the advantage over Tarleton's troops.

Thick woods stretched along one side and a strong rail fence along the other. The house stood on a steep hill that sloped down to the Tyger River, which ran along the back. In front, the road wound up another hill where Tarleton was gathering his soldiers.

Sumter had not allowed his men to stop for food or water. Now they built a fire of twigs and dead branches to cook meat and bake wads of dough on the ends of long sticks, cut from nearby bushes.

While they were eating, a lady galloped into camp. Mary Dillard lived six miles south of Blackstock's. She had seen a British line of soldiers march by her home. Brought before Sumter, she blurted out, "The British are coming!"

"Do they have fieldpieces?" Sumter asked.

"Only men on horseback," she answered.

Eager to be prepared, Sumter positioned his colonels and their troops to the best advantage against the enemy.

From inside the Blackstock home, family members watched Sumter's maneuvers. Mary Blackstock's husband was away fighting with another regiment. Spunky and brave, Mary threw a shawl around her shoulders and went out to confront Sumter.

"General," she exclaimed tartly, "I won't have any fighting around my house."

But Mary Blackstock was too late. Tarleton was already headed their way with plans to pin Sumter's men against the Tyger River while he waited for his artillery. And the Gamecock's feathers were ruffled. He was ready for a fight.

As Tarleton's dragoons stood ready on the hill, awaiting the command, Sumter ordered a colonel and 400 infantrymen to charge them.

The troops obeyed and began firing. But they were too far away to make their shots count. As they struggled to reload their muskets, British bayonets cut them down. Survivors raced toward the woods.

British soldiers drew closer. The Patriots opened fire. Sumter ordered a colonel to lead a sneak attack on the idle dragoons watching the fight. Then he galloped directly into battle.

As the struggle raged, a small band of Patriots positioned themselves close enough to fire off buckshot, tumbling twenty enemy soldiers from their saddles.

The British were falling so fast, both sides stumbled over dead horses and men. Tarleton had no choice but to retreat.

Sumter spurred his horse forward to get a

better look at the retreating enemy. One of Tarleton's men spotted the general's blue coat and took a shot.

Sumter glimpsed the shooter just as he fired. In that split second, the general jerked sideways to protect his heart. Five buckshot ripped into his chest. Another plunged into his right shoulder, chipping a splinter from his backbone and coming to rest in his left shoulder. Sumter gritted his teeth and rode into camp.

Aides helped the general dismount. One heard a noise among the dry leaves. Turning, he saw a stream of blood trickling down Sumter's coat and spattering on the ground.

"General!" he cried. "You are wounded!"

"Say nothing about it," Sumter replied. Then he asked that his horse be led to shelter. Realizing he was too weak to continue, Sumter ordered

Colonel Twiggs to assume command.

The general's aides helped him to the Blackstock house. Scarcely able to speak, he whispered to Soldier Tom, "I'm badly wounded. Get a doctor."

A doctor, pulled from the field, quickly realized Sumter was bleeding to death. "Grab the bedposts," he instructed, "and hold on."

The doctor dug to remove the buckshot, stopped the bleeding, and dressed the wound.

Left in command, Colonel Twiggs sent a militia to follow the retreating Tarleton. Then soldiers rescued the wounded from both sides and took them into the Blackstock home to be given aid.

Tarleton had been defeated.

At nightfall soldiers placed the barely conscious Gamecock on a crude litter. Guarded by other soldiers, they crept down the hill through a chilling rain to carry Sumter to Colonel Watson's home on Sugar Creek.

With Soldier Tom caring for him and the militia of New Acquisition standing guard, Sumter recovered.

# 11.
# Calling It Quits

When Sumter was growing up, he always insisted on being the leader. As an adult, that did not change. He never liked taking orders from other officers, not even from the commander of the Southern army. While Sumter recovered, General Nathanael Greene replaced General Gates as commander.

Though Sumter still suffered from his battle wounds, he again took command of his militia. He even talked some Tory prisoners into joining his troops.

Eager to get back into action, the Gamecock decided he could take the British fort set up at the

Granby farmhouse. Without waiting for orders, he sent General Greene a message that he was confident of a victory there. Sumter was in the process of carrying out his plans when Greene sent General Henry Lee, known as Light Horse Harry, to assume command of the operation.

Sumter's anger flared. He grew even angrier when, in his brief absence, Lee allowed the British to surrender Fort Granby. Sumter had his heart set on taking the fort in battle and he felt Lee had cheated him of the honor. In a fit of rage he sent a letter of resignation to General Greene.

Even though Greene had been angered when Sumter refused to obey his orders, he knew many soldiers depended on Sumter for leadership.

In response to the Gamecock's resignation Greene wrote:

The Honourable Brigadier General Sumter
Dear Sir:

I take the liberty to return your commission and to inform you I cannot accept it and beg you to continue.

I am sorry for your ill health [referring to Sumter's rifle wounds]. I don't have to tell you how important your services are to this country. I have confidence in your abilities.

With esteem and respect,
Your most obedient humble servant,
Nathanael Greene

With his anger softened, Sumter reconsidered and set about once again plundering Tory plantations and paying his men with possessions they seized.

Although Greene did not agree with Sumter's plundering, he allowed him to carry out what had become known as "Sumter's Law." In this way Sumter could provide pay to soldiers who received no money for fighting. As well as clothing, food, medicine, and animals, the plunder included slaves.

After his men were paid, Sumter carried out Greene's order to destroy all remaining British forts. Later, however, he failed to follow Greene's command to "get in front of Lord Rawdon's army" as they marched toward Ninety Six where Greene's troops tried to force the British from Star Fort.

Greene's message ordered Sumter to "scorch the land" and destroy all food and provisions the Tory army might live on as they marched. When Greene sent a second message, repeating his command, Sumter responded that many of his men had gone home to protect their families.

Sumter liked the challenge of a fight. General Greene once called him a "glory fighter" for the reckless way he led his men into battle.

In spite of his fearlessness and his tireless energy, the long years of war had been a struggle for Sumter mentally and physically. He continued to suffer from his old shoulder wounds. The musket ball he received at Hanging Rock was never removed from his thigh. He also suffered from chronic malaria.

On January 2, 1782, Sumter made his final report to Greene. Then he bade farewell to the backwoodsmen he had enlisted, trained, and led for eighteen months.

As he said goodbye, Sumter recalled scenes of his men charging with homemade swords and squirrel rifles. He thought of the brothers and cousins lying dead on the battlefield. In the end, he could not hold back the tears.

# 12.
# A Hero Returns Home

Sumter returned to his home on the Great Savannah where he again enjoyed Mary's attention and companionship. After a few weeks of rest, he rode to Jacksonboro to take his seat on the General Assembly. Many of the generals he had served with were there.

Governor Rutledge spoke to the group of reunited veterans, praising them all. He noted special gratitude to Sumter and Francis Marion. "With a small number of men," he said, "they continued to harass and defeat large parties."

Rutledge also honored General Nathanael Greene and the bravery of the men under his command.

One of the main problems the Assembly faced was how to handle the Tories now that the Patriots had won the war. It was suggested that slaves be seized from the Tories and given to soldiers who had received no pay for their military service.

Marion had never been in favor of "Sumter's Law." Now he spoke angrily against such practices. He believed the Assembly should work at getting along with these Americans who had taken the British side in the war.

No decision was made about the slaves. However, the Tories were punished. Patriots seized property of the Tories who had been most violent. Others were forced to leave the country.

Unhappy that the Assembly had not come up with a way to pay his soldiers, Sumter resigned his commission as brigadier general and returned home.

The British had spared his home on the Great Savannah, but Sumter's slaves were gone, his horses stolen, and his cattle slaughtered. With the courage of an old war hero, Sumter set to work and was soon planting crops again.

He began to take an interest in the government of the colonies and was elected to the Continental Congress.

When the bitterness between the Patriots and the Loyalists began to calm, Sumter realized that peace would bring about growth. Imagining crossroads growing into villages, he bought thousands of acres of land.

On his plantation in the High Hills north of Stateburg he built a large house he called Home House. He welcomed all to his home—including Indians and fellow soldiers.

He even entertained his old boyhood friend Lucas. They talked of their days plowing, cockfighting, and playing games of skill.

"Ah," Sumter told Lucas, "that was in our youthful days."

Now, he took a great deal of interest in helping others. He served in his church and donated property to it for a new building. Because of his own lack of formal education, he wanted to give others an opportunity to learn. He helped open a seminary at Stateburg. He pushed for

dredging and digging canals around the state to make travel and transportation of goods easier.

The citizens of his district urged him into national politics. As a United States congressman, Sumter set off to Richmond, Virginia, the country's capital at that time. He traveled in the style of a gentleman with his coachman and personal body servant. As a congressman, he fought for states rights.

On occasion his granddaughter Louisa, who attended school in Pennsylvania, accompanied him. On their way back home from one trip, he took Louisa by his boyhood home at Preddy's Creek, Virginia.

Pointing out a meadow, he told her, "I used to tend sheep there when I was a boy."

Sumter's old wounds bothered him less as he grew older. "Thomas is seventy," a friend remarked, "and he still vaults into his saddle and rides his horse with ease."

At home Sumter was nearly always on horseback. He visited neighbors with whom he gossiped and argued politics. Often he joined in games with young people. They all loved him.

As the last of the surviving Revolutionary War generals, Sumter honored others by his presence. His church congregation rose when he entered and remained standing until he was seated.

The Sumters had a good life together during these years. But when Mary died of yellow fever at the age of ninety-four, Sumter left Home House for another of his plantations near Camden. His son Thomas and Thomas's family of seven children moved into Home House.

Sumter later moved to South Mount, another of his plantations. He turned the first floor of the home into a store offering everything from coon skins to cotton. His grandchildren loved visiting him there.

With Soldier Tom as his companion, he toured old battle sites. Sons and grandsons of the men who fought by his side welcomed him into their homes as a hero.

At age ninety-seven Sumter still rode his horse. He had become a legend. A news reporter sent to cover a court case at Bradford Springs almost forgot his assignment when he saw General Sumter. "Everyone wanted to shake the hand that wielded the sword of liberty," he wrote of the occasion.

A grandson named for Sumter often rode horseback with the old general through the hills of hickories, oaks, and maples. On the morning of June 1, 1832, Sumter had his horse saddled early for a ride with his grandson. He puttered around in his apple orchard, trimming a branch here and there, while he waited. Suddenly he called to a slave standing nearby, "I am tired." Soon he was dead.

A simple funeral took place at Home House where Thomas Sumter was buried beside Mary. Mourners placed a monument at his grave, which reads:

This stone marks the grave of one of South
Carolina's most distinguished citizens,
Thomas Sumter
One of the founders of the Republic.
Born in Va., Aug. 14, 1734
Died June 1, 1832

He came to South Carolina about 1760
and was in the Indian service on the
Frontier for several years before settling
as a planter in this vicinity.
Commandant of 6th Regt., S.C. Line,
Continental Estab., 1776-1778.
Brig. Gen. S.C. Militia, 1780-1782.
Member of Continental Congress, 1783-1784.
Member of U.S. Congress, 1789-1793, 1797-1801.
U.S. Senator, 1801-1810

Tanto Nomini Nullum
Par Elogium

GEORGIA

South
Carolina

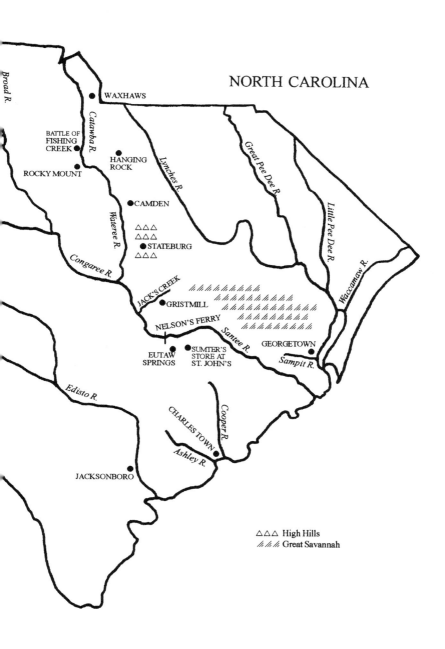

# Words Needed for Understanding

*abatis*      a barricade made from trees, placed with sharpened branches directed toward the enemy

*ambush*      a war tactic in which persons in hiding make a surprise attack on the enemy

*bind*      to assign as an apprentice

*bombarded*      to attack continuously with weapons

*breeches*      trousers reaching the knees

*brigade*      a group of military persons

*campaign*      a military expedition

*cavalry*      combat troops mounted on horses

*chronic*      recurring often over a long period of time

*Continental*      relating to a soldier of the American colonies during the Revolutionary War

*dragoons*      soldiers who fought on horseback

*dredging*      deepening harbors or canals

*epaulettes*      shoulder ornaments on military uniforms

| | |
|---|---|
| *epidemic* | a disease that spreads through a community |
| *escort* | to go with; to accompany |
| *fieldpiece* | movable artillery; a gun suitable for use on the battlefield |
| *flounce* | to turn quickly |
| *ford* | a shallow place in a stream or river |
| *forge* | a place where metal is heated and hammered |
| *gamecock* | a male chicken (rooster) bred for fighting |
| *garrison* | troops stationed in a fort |
| *genteel* | showing politeness and refinement |
| *gristmill* | a mill where grain is ground into meal or flour |
| *guerrilla warfare* | military actions carried out by groups under cover, designed to harass and weaken the enemy |
| *guineas* | English gold coins |
| *hampered* | kept from moving |

| | |
|---|---|
| *harass* | to trouble by repeated raids or attacks |
| *headstrong* | determined not to follow orders |
| *johnny cake* | a bread made of oatmeal or coarse wheat flour, baked on a griddle |
| *kindling* | small pieces of wood easily lighted |
| *loot* | plunder; to take by force |
| *Loyalists* | colonists who remained loyal to the British government; also called Tories |
| *malaria* | a disease believed to be carried by mosquitoes |
| *maneuvers* | planned movements of troops |
| *midwife* | a woman assisting in childbirth |
| *militia* | a volunteer group of soldiers, usually made up of ordinary citizens |
| *New Acquisition* | a settlement in the Carolina colony |
| *Patriots* | colonists who believed in America's right to independence from England; one who supports his or her country |
| *penetrate* | to pass through |

| | |
|---|---|
| *plunder* | to destroy property and take goods by force |
| *proclamation* | an order by one with official authority |
| *prosperous* | rich |
| *provisions* | food and other supplies gathered and stored for future needs |
| *reputation* | what others think of you |
| *respectable* | worthy of honor |
| *riddled* | covered with many holes |
| *scarlet* | a shade of red |
| *seminary* | a school for higher learning |
| *strategy* | a plan of action for a large scale military operation |
| *tactics* | plans of action in war |
| *vault* | to jump or spring from one position to another |
| *wield* | to handle and use a tool with skill |

# Things to Do and Think About

1. Make a large map as a class project. Put in major rivers and Revolutionary War battle sites, as well as other places relating to your study.

2. Compare your childhood to Sumter's. It was said that Sumter always wanted to be the leader in any game he played. How do you feel about that?

3. Do you know that Christopher Gadsden's followers became known as the Liberty Party and they held meetings under a giant oak in Charleston? The tree became known as the Liberty Tree. Sons of the American Revolution placed a marker near the site where the tree stood. What part did Gadsden play in Sumter's becoming a Patriot?

4. This book mentions the fighting of gamecocks. This is a cruel practice and is now against the law. Can you think of any other cruel activities involving animals?

5. If you have not already read the biography of Francis Marion, do so and then tell the ways

Marion and Sumter were alike as well as how they differed.

6. What was the Provincial Congress?

7. In the battle of Rocky Mount soldiers made what we might think of as bullet-proof vests. How was that done?

8. Try to locate modern-day cities at or near the sites of places mentioned in this book.

9. What was the difference in the militias which Sumter and Marion led and the Continental Army?

10. Because the British still held Charleston, the South Carolina legislature met at the village of Jacksonboro in the Low Country. A marker on US Highway 17 near Jacksonboro states that Patriots passed confiscation and amercement acts there after the war was over. Can you explain what these acts allowed?

11. Sumter participated in battles not mentioned in this story. Would you like to find out where they were?

12. Both sides, Tories (also called Loyalists) and Patriots, plundered and burned during the Revolutionary War. However, some officers had a reputation for going too far. British Colonel Banastre Tarleton's brutal massacres were often referred to as "Tarleton's Quarter" because he was said to kill soldiers who surrendered. Thomas Sumter's plundering and looting coined the expression "Sumter's Law." Can you explain what that meant?

13. The monument at Sumter's grave includes the Latin words **par elogium tanto Nomini Nullum.** The words are taken from the tomb of Machiavelli, an Italian statesman and writer. The English translation is "Eulogy can add nothing to so great a name." What do you think the quotation means?

14. Choose a person from this book. Pretend to be that person and give a brief monologue on why you acted the way you did in a particular situation.

15. Write skits of different scenes in this book. Have several classmates help you act them out for the class.

# Sources Used

Bass, Robert D. *Gamecock: The Life and Campaigns of General Thomas Sumter.* New York: Holt, Rinehart and Winston, 1961.

——. *Swamp Fox: The Life and Campaigns of General Francis Marion.* Lexington, SC: Sandlapper Press, 1974.

Edgar, Walter. *South Carolina: A History.* Columbia, SC: University of South Carolina Press, 1998.

Hilborn, Nat, and Sam Hilborn. *Battleground of Freedom.* Columbia, SC: Sandlapper Press, 1970.

Jones, Lewis P. *South Carolina: One of Fifty States.* Orangeburg, SC: Sandlapper Publishing Company, Inc., 1985.

McGrady, Edward. *History of South Carolina in the Revolution.* 2 vols. New York: The Macmillan Company, 1901.

Ripley, Warren. *Battleground: South Carolina in the Revolution.* Charleston, SC: Evening Post Publishing Company, 1983.

Thane, Elswyth. *The Fighting Quaker: Nathanael Greene*. New York: Aeonian Press, Inc. 1972.

Wallace, David Duncan. *South Carolina: A Short History, 1520-1948*. Columbia, SC: University of South Carolina Press, 1966.

Weigley, Russell F. *The Partisan War: The Campaign of 1780-1782*. Columbia, SC: University of South Carolina Press, 1970.

## About the Author

Idella Bodie was born in Ridge Spring, South Carolina. She received her degree in English from Columbia College and taught high school English and creative writing for thirty-one years.

Ms. Bodie visits many schools each year where she talks with students about writing. She also leads writing workshops for adults.

Idella Bodie lives in Aiken with her husband Jim. When she is not busy with research, writing, or public appearances, Ms. Bodie enjoys reading and gardening.

# Books by Idella Bodie